T0015347

GAY GIRL PRAYERS

EMILY AUSTIN

GAY GIRL PRAYERS

BRICK BOOKS

Library and Archives Canada Cataloguing in Publication
Title: Gay girl prayers / Emily Austin.
Names: Austin, Emily R., author.
Identifiers: Canadiana (print) 20230583032 | Canadiana (ebook) 20230583040 |
ISBN 9781771316224 (softcover) | ISBN 9781771316231 (EPUB) |
ISBN 9781771316248 (PDF)
Subjects: LCGFT: Poetry.
Classification: LCC PS8601.U88 g39 2024 | DDC c811/.6—DC23

We gratefully acknowledge the Canada Council for the Arts, the Government
of Canada through the Canada Book Fund, and the Ontario Arts Council and
the Government of Ontario for their support of our publishing program.

Edited by River Halen.
Author photo by Bridget Forberg.
Cover photo © Walker Art Library / Alamy Stock Photo.
The book is set in Family and Lyyra.
Design by Natalie Olsen, Kisscut Design.

lb

BRICK BOOKS

487 King St. W.
Kingston, Ontario
K7L 2X7
www.brickbooks.ca

Though much of the work of Brick Books takes place on the ancestral lands
of the Anishinaabeg, Haudenosaunee, Huron-Wendat, and Mississaugas of the
Credit peoples, our editors, authors, and readers from many backgrounds are
situated from coast to coast to coast in Canada on the traditional and unceded
territories of over six hundred nations who have cared for Turtle Island from
time immemorial. While living and working on these lands, we are committed
to hearing and returning the rightful imaginative space to the poetries, songs,
and stories that have been untold, under-told, wrongly told, and suppressed
through colonization.

FOR ANYONE TAUGHT THEY
WERE GOING TO HELL.

CONTENTS

GAY GIRL PRAYERS

Strange women,
darkness remains dark
until there is light—
so, smoke a cigarette
and listen to the beast roar.

Shall we resurrect, strange women?
Rise like steam, like birds from a subway station?
Defy the convention of the proverbs?
Write with our fingers?
I am.

Resurrect the spirit,
fly into the ember,
caw a song in the air
like a crow.

I am who I am,
she is who she is,
you are who you are.
Can you hear me?
Are you listening?

I am sweltering.
Rainbows arched in the sky,
ink in our skin.
I am.

Naked under gold and pearls
a volcano erupts.
Take the pew,
she is at the pulpit.
She is.

Take the white clouds into white rooms.
She is at the front now,
fire in Her belly,
fruit on Her chin.

There are words in Her mouth,
in Her gut with the apple.
We listen to the crack of fire,
burning bushes
        crack
listen.

There are virgins in the white clouds
waiting for dead men
        crack
if heaven is hell for girls
        crack
then heaven is hell.

Keep your soul insurance in the fountain
        crack
there is a shadow poisoning the well.

Wet your hair with drops of the night
        crack, crack
praise the monsters,
meet me where the fire never goes out.

CRACK, CRACK

If they try to strip you
of your technicolor robes
show them how the sun
the moon
the stars
all kneel to Queens

GENESIS 37

Truly I tell you,
if you have pride
as small as a mustard seed,
you can say to a mountain,
"Move from here to there,"
and it will move.

MATTHEW 17:20

I am lying
with strange women
in torn clothing
my blood is wine
and I am eating Madeleines

I have drawn on my skin

a triangle
a nautical star
a stalk of lavender
two men making out
the eleventh letter of the Greek alphabet
a unicorn and the words:

If ghosts exist
my body turns to stardust
If ghosts do not exist
I do

LEVITICUS 18-20

Heaven is ten girls
who take their lamps
to one another's bed chambers
to light their rooms
until they sleep.

MATTHEW 25:1

You were created in the image of God—
man and woman, God created you
so, man and woman God must be.

The holy spirit is hovering.
She is fluttering over the face of the waters,
she came to earth in the body of a son.

Do not forget the rock who begot you.
He gave birth to you
because fathers can give birth.

Change the bread into flesh,
change the wine into blood—
sacred bodies transubstantiate.

Use a chalice rather than a cup.
A chalice is a godly kind of vessel,
a hallowed beaker for transcendent blood.

DEUTERONOMY 32:18 & JOHN 6:35

Hail Jeff,
blessed are thou among men
and blessed is the fruit of thy seed, Judy
pray for us

THE VIRGIN JEFF

Don't forgive me
I haven't sinned
in my thoughts
or in my words
in the strange things I have done
in the ordinary things I have failed to do
through my heart
through my heart
through my heart

ACT OF PRIDE

Those who lie with men
as men lie with a woman
inherit heaven

Take off the grave clothes
nothing abominable is attractive
you are altogether beautiful

There is no flaw

LEVITICUS 20:13

Don't take this, any of you, and eat it—
this is her body.

Don't take this, any of you, and drink it—
this is her blood, which pumps for its own ends.

Faster when she's nervous,
when she's buying shirts from the men's section

or shopping at PinkCherry,
when she locks eyes with a woman wearing a carabiner,

when there is a passing mention of queer people in media,
like when a cartoon character has two dads.

Slower when she's explaining there hasn't been a mistake at the hotel
when the room for her and a woman has one bed,

when she looks over her shoulder at dusk
while holding hands with someone who isn't a man.

Faster again when she clocks a queer kid
and says your hair looks cool.

WORDS OF CONSECRATION

Her desire will be
for whatever she's into.
If she wants it to hurt,
she'll ask.

She doesn't need to multiply anything
to fill her quiver
or be fruitful.

GENESIS 3:16 & GENESIS 9:7

Heaven is ten girls
who take their lamps
to each other's bed chambers
to read lesbian erotica
and make out.

MATTHEW 25:2

She is not a lily among brambles
waiting to be led to still waters.
bless her if she is perverse and wayward,
cunning.
Bless her if she pleases herself.

SONG OF SOLOMON 2:2

Ghosts visit girls at nighttime
come upon them in their sleep
try to turn them into vessels
into servants

Ghosts find girls are as empty
as the Red Sea at high tide
as the inns were in Bethlehem
as the earth on the seventh day
as the trees were in Eden
as the tabernacles during Ordinary Time
as the baskets when Jesus fed the multitude
as a thurible teeming with incense

They are in servitude to no spirit
but their own

LUKE 1:26-38

If the power of the flame draws those
who gaze at stars,
at new moons,
it will not burn them.
Behold, God made them enchanting,
strange, and incombustible,
like water.

Read the lines on your palms.
Ask the stars; ask the dead.
Fortune tellers know
thou shalt relish a witch to live.

EXODUS 22:18 & ISAIAH 43:2

Heaven is ten girls
who take their lamps
to each other's bed chambers
to consider polyamory
and sperm donors.

MATTHEW 25:3

Take the stones you plan to throw at her
for not screaming
or not screaming loudly enough
while she was raped
put them inside of your pockets
and walk on water

DEUTERONOMY 22:23-27

As you did it
to the strangest
of my sisters
you did it to me

MATTHEW 25:40

I presented myself, as a living offering, to Rebecca.
I offered my body to Tamar and Abigail,
my blood to Miriam and Deborah.
I gave my reasonable service to Rehab
and to Hannah, Mary, and Ruth,
who all sacrificed a lot
to offer their bodies to me
and their spirits to themselves.

ROMANS 12:1

1 **T**wo angels disguised as humans pulled over in the city of Sodom. They were on their way to heaven but needed to stretch their legs, use the washroom, and grab a bite to eat.

2 That evening, the men of Sodom were drunk and rowdy. It was a statutory holiday, and there was a football game on. That, coupled with the fact that Sodom was notorious for having a disquieting number of men's rights activists, created an inhospitable environment for many day-trippers, and for most folks taking rest stops off the highway.

3 When the men of Sodom spotted the angels, they started shouting f-slurs. This is because the angels looked clean, fashionable, and pretty, and men in Sodom associated that with homosexuality. They didn't realize those qualities happened to be linked with celestial beings.

4 Before the angels could get back to their car, the men of Sodom surrounded them. They yelled at them to suck their dicks. It was difficult to tell whether they were joking, or whether they actually wanted to receive rape-blow-jobs; however, Lot, a local vicar, thought they were definitely being serious.

That dismayed him—not because he took an issue with rape; he was also a rapist himself—but because his religion was homophobic. So, he shouted, "Come on, guys! Don't be gay! That's gross! I have two virgin daughters right over here. Wouldn't you rather assault my girls?"

5 There were two teenagers standing near him. They had their arms crossed. They looked freaked out. One said, "What the fuck, Dad?"

6 The crowd of men paused. One put his hand to his chest and said, "Wow, that is so charitable of you, Lot."

7 Another said, "Damn. What a nice guy, eh? Offering up his virgin daughters. That is incredibly big of you, sir."

8 "What a hospitable dude."

9 While Lot was being praised, and carried around on the men's shoulders, the angels asked the girls, "Are you two okay?"

10 The girls said, "No, our dad is obviously an incestuous pedophile. Can you please take us somewhere safe?"

11 The angels nodded, "Yes, for sure. We'll take you to the gay bar in heaven."

GENESIS 19 & HEBREWS 13:2

This is where he was baptized,
his head held down under water.
He didn't drown,
but he wasn't born again.

He was born again when he met Matthew,
Mark, Luke, and John,
who held his head down in their laps,
stroked his hair, and lifted his gaze
to heaven.

JOHN 3:1-21

Heaven is two girls
who take their lamps
to their shared bed chambers
to call their mutual ex-girlfriend
to ask what's new?
How are you?
Do you want to grab lunch tomorrow?
I was thinking of your mom the other day.
How is Mary? Tell Mary I said hi.
I'm here with Delilah. Do you want to talk to Delilah?
Okay, here she is.
Bye, I love you too.

MATTHEW 25:4

If you are ever forced to conceive of anything,
by a condom or a government that fails you,
by a Tinder date who ghosts you,
by God, your father, or by some unholy spirit,
let it be that you are important and good, like Mary
but with more choice.

MATTHEW 1:18

This isn't the hill she wanted to die on,
but she will be damned
before others pass here.

She'll climb on her cross at Easter dinner
while her homophobic uncle serves sour wine.
She'll call her cousin out when that cousin says something hateful.
She'll say, "Mom, they know what they're doing."

She will rise from her chair,
contemplate going through hell to forgive them,
ascend to the room she prepared for herself,
and find peace in the miracle of her life.

AT CALVARY

Your mother came naked from her mother's womb
and returned there gutted

Cover yourself in a golden chamois
return to the forest adorned

JOB 1:21

Jesus's great-grandmother was a harlot and a saint
she was virtuous and worthy
not because of the time she hid men in her rafters
to help them escape
but because she was intrinsically valuable
sacred like all sex workers
like all people
like you

JOSHUA 2

Heaven is ten strange girls
who take emulsion and sensitizer
to their basements
to screen print T-shirts
with the text:

If God hates gays
why are we so cute?

MATTHEW 25:5

A strange woman
is a bright sky
a catholic goldmine
an angel's quarry

Her steps take hold on heaven
follow her

PROVERBS 22:14 & PROVERBS 5:3-5

If some guy asks who you belong to
while you're sowing your oats with women,
answer Ruth, if Ruth is your name.

RUTH 2:5

He was fingering dirt
in his castle
while he watched her

He was unclean
when he took her

foul as always
when he left

                              She was bathing in the moonlight
                                       when he saw her

                                       She was spotless
                                       when he took her

                                       clean as always
                                       when he left

2 SAMUEL 11

1 **N**ewborn enbies are the crown of old fruitcakes;
    the glory of baby gays
        is in their daddies.
2 Fairies are the pride of their aunt Dorothy;
    butches are a blessing
        to femmes, stones,
3 pansies, other butches, and androgynes.
    They are a splendour
        to earth's garden.
4 Trans kids are the joy of their elders,
    and their sports teams.
        Every fruit is a blessing.

PROVERBS 17:6

Heaven is two women
who take their phones
to their shared bedroom,
scroll and laugh sporadically
as they flash each other pictures of toads,
and say, "Honey, this reminds me of you."

MATTHEW 25:6

Name the vessel stronger
than the one that brought you
and every person who is
and ever was
to life

1 PETER 3:7

Let me kiss her
with the kisses of my mouth—
for her love is better than the apple boughs in blossom.

Because of the savour of lavender ointments,
her name is as ointment poured forth;
therefore, do strange girls love her.

Draw me through the glades of poppies,
we will run after her—
the queen hath brought me into her chambers.

I will be glad and rejoice,
I will remember this love—
the perverts want her.

They made her keeper of the violets,
but her own violets have not been woven
into garlands or a crown.

Tell me, where dost she sleep?
Where dost she nod
to drones of bees at noontide?

I have compared her, my love,
to the company of unicorns in Sappho's Garden
to the grotto cool of the nymphs.

A bundle of myrrh is my beloved unto me.
She shall lie all night betwixt my breasts,
bruised the red blood of roses.

My beloved is unto me
as a cluster of green carnations
in the gardens at Mytilene.

She is strange, she is strange, my love.
She hast yearnful eyes,
tresses long.

Our bed is orange, pink, and purple
for, lo, the winter is past,
the flood is over.

Moss and flowers
appeared on the earth
the black swans have come.

O my spouse, she who cometh from the wilderness.
Love prevails because it is as life-giving as water,
more perilous than death; it never waits.

Let my beloved into my garden.
Let her eat pleasant fruits,
wear crowns of roses and crocuses.

I found her whom my soul loveth.
I held her and would not let her go.
My beloved is mine and I am hers.

SONG OF SHULAMIT

Heaven is ten girls
who take their lamps
to their friend's bed chambers
to bring them soup
and feel their forehead
when they're sick.

MATTHEW 25:7

If authority is granted by order
and Adam was formed before Eve
then suffer not a man to teach
nor usurp authority over dust
but to be in silence—
for dust was formed first, then Adam.

GENESIS 2:7 & 1 TIMOTHY 2:13

Families are focused on
and children are saved
when drag kings and queens
read picture books about gay penguins
wrapping their wings around an egg
with the pinions and plumage of love.

PSALM 91

The price of a man was fifty shekels
while the price of a woman was thirty
but the price of Judas was thirty also
so that is their cost of everything

LEVITICUS 27:3-4 & MATTHEW 26:14-16

In the name of the questioning,
the curious,
and the closeted.

Glory be to the butches,
the studs,
and the femmes.

In the name of the aces,
the demisexual,
and the gray.

Glory be to bisexuals,
pansexuals,
and the fluid.

In the name of trans lesbians,
T4Ts, non-binary bisexuals,
and all queer trans people.

Glory be to the intersex,
all gay men, witches,
and bears.

THE SIGN OF THE CROSS

Hey Mamma
who art in a lesbian bar,
hallowed be thy yearning.
Thy drag kingdom come,
thy strap undone
with femmes as it is with butches.
Give us our daily oat milk,
forgive us our baby gay phase
as we forgive God and her misled toadies.
Lead us not into bigoted churches,
deliver us from conservative politicians.

HEY MAMMA

Heaven is ten girls
who take their lamps
to each other's bed chambers
to have an orgy
until a phone rings
and a girl gets bad news
and the room surrounds her.
They put their hands on her shoulders
and say, "We're here for you."
"We'll help."

MATTHEW 25:8

Don't break your chest for me
if I were made of ribs
dry rubbed in sugar and spices
I might love you for it
but I existed in the previous verse
and I like eating fruit and being smart
so don't hurt yourself
I will only ever love dirt and my chosen family

GENESIS 2:22

Though Delilah's hair was a covering,
a veil to keep her modest,
a cloth to wash your feet,
she too was born with superpower strength.

It grows from her armpits, her arms, her legs,
from the tissue that covers her pubic bone,
from her face, her stomach, her feet.

It grows from the bare patches in her eyebrows,
from her bald or shaven head.

1 CORINTHIANS 11:1-6 & LUKE 7:36-50 & JUDGES 16:17

Lot's unnamed daughters had an unnamed mother.
She was turned to salt for looking backwards.
At nighttime, before the girls slept,
they must have talked about her.
"Should we keep her salty body?"
"How will we remember her without pictures?"
"Cameras don't exist yet."
Maybe they hummed songs she sang,
or made recipes she taught them.
Maybe they saw her in their dreams,
or wrote poems about her face and wonders.
Could girls write back then?
How did they remember her?
How do we remember them?

Spit on the ground,
put the mud in your eyes.

JOHN 9:1-12

The natural use of a person's body
is to carry their heart and brain.

Let there be light in the vaults of the sky,
let the water teem with living creatures.

Let there be elderly queer men in movie theatres,
eating popcorn, laughing loudly at previews.

Let non-binary parents nap on the beach
while their kids bury them up to their necks in sand.

Let dykes offer crows hazelnuts and cranberries
until the crows bring them buttons and bones.

Winged birds fly, wild animals roam,
seeds and plants sprout.

Look upon that and all that has been made
and see that it is good.

ROMANS 1:26-27

His soul is bound to the soul of another,
and he loves him as his own soul.

He shall leave his parents
and be joined to his husband.

The two shall become one flesh.
Let no one separate.

Love is proud.

2 SAMUEL 1:26 & MATTHEW 19:4-6

Ruth said to Naomi,
"Entreat me not to leave you,
or to turn back from following after you;
for wherever you go, I will U-Haul;
your people shall be my chosen family,
your clothes, my clothes,
your God, my God;
where you die, I will die,
there will I be buried,
and theologians will write that we were friends,
travelling companions,
but I will have loved you
with the purest desires of my heart."

ROMANS 1:26-27 & RUTH 1:16

There is grace in men having long hair
grace in women shearing their heads

My godmother is wearing a wrestling singlet
my godfather is wearing a silk trumpet gown

DEUTERONOMY 22:5 & 1 CORINTHIANS 11:6 & 11:14

Here I am
the mother of your mothers
tell the others
I am on fire
and I am who I am

EXODUS 3:14

Thou art worthy,
O queer folk,
for thou hast made:

- teleidoscopes
- modern science
- computers
- search engines
- erotic pop art
- sex toys
- the cure to sleeping sickness
- flowerpots made out of toilets dumped outside lesbian bars
- Pride parades
- a sensor to detect early-stage pancreatic cancer
- Grindr
- the *Mona Lisa*

- safer spaces
- dance films
- every funny tweet
- "Bohemian Rhapsody"
- "Fast Car"
- riots
- poetry
- mistakes
- families
- blood
- spit
- sweat
- tears
- carbon dioxide

There was a bright star in the sky
the night you were born.

REVELATION 4:11

Long lay the world in error pining
'til strange girls felt worth

A thrill of hope
weary folks rejoice

Yonder breaks
a new and glorious morn

Stand on your feet

O HOLY NIGHT

She is as brilliant as jasper or carnelian
give her our gifts
protect her

MATTHEW 2

Do you hear what I hear?
Heaven and Nature are singing
they're drag queens
they're harmonizing
queer joy to the world
while two men slow dance
and I read a text from my friend
who is four months on T
sharing their name is Felix now
which means happy
repeat the sounding joy
there is a character who is bi on prime-time TV
and a Pride flag at City Hall
repeat, repeat
there's a queer picture book display at the library
a kid is picking one out, his dad is smiling
saying, "That's a good pick, buddy"
and I'm going to tell someone I love them
and they're going to tell me they love me back
and we're going to get married and immaculately conceive a baby
with our two holy spirits and a turkey baster
or maybe we won't
maybe I'll just write a poem about that person I love
that gay people might feel happy reading
and when I'm grey I'll remember them fondly
think of how lucky I am to have loved someone
and hum Heaven and Nature's song

JOY TO THE WORLD

Heaven is all strange people
who take their lamps
to their bed chambers
to say good night,
I love you.

MATTHEW 25:9

ACKNOWLEDGMENTS

Thank you to my family and friends—especially, for this book, my friend Matthew. I would endure Catholic school all over again to find you and your technicolour dream coat, Matt.

Thank you, River Halen, who thoughtfully edited this book and drastically improved it. Let's just say there would have been no mention of turkey basters if not for River's editorial talents. Truly, the best lines in this book were suggested by them. I am very lucky to have had such a gifted poet and editor work on this with me. Thank you so much, sincerely, River.

Thank you to everyone at Brick Books, including Alayna Munce, Brenda Leifso, Nick Thran, and Sonnet L'Abbé. Thank you also to everyone who has supported any of my writing, including Heather Carr, Daniella Wexler, Jade Hui, Loan Le, Gena Lanzi, Isabel DaSilva, Jillian Levick, Kirsty Doole, Aimee Oliver-Powell, Bobby Mostyn-Owen, Kate Straker, Sophie Walker, Kelli McAdams, Cayley Pimentel, Sarah St. Pierre, Janie Yoon, the Friedrich Agency, and many others.

Thank you to my English teachers.

Thank you to Lucy Dacus for the song "VBS."

Thank you to the folks on Bookstagram and BookTok.

Thank you to Bridget, who isn't big into poetry but still let me read these out loud to her. Thanks also to Lou.

Thank you to the Catholic Church for the trauma.

I wrote these poems with a grant from the Canada Council for the Arts. In addition to affording me the time to write, their support gave me the personal encouragement one needs to share poetry.

Lastly, thank you to anyone reading this. I am earnestly grateful to anyone who has spent time reading anything I've written.

EMILY AUSTIN was born in St. Thomas, Ontario, Canada. She studied English literature, religious studies, and library science at King's University College and Western University. She has received two writing grants from the Canada Council for the Arts, and she has written two novels (*Everyone in this Room Will Someday Be Dead* and *Interesting Facts About Space*.) Emily currently lives in Ottawa in the territory of the Anishinaabe Algonquin Nation.

MIX
Paper
FSC® C100212

Printed by Imprimerie Gauvin
Gatineau, Québec